Thorazine Ice Cream Parlor

Poems by Denmark Laine

Kansas City   Spartan Press   Missouri

Spartan Press
Kansas City, MO
spartanpresskc@gmail.com

Copyright © Denmark Laine, 2019
First Edition 1 3 5 7 9 10 8 6 4 2
ISBN: 978-1-950380-02-2
LCCN: 2019932564

Design, edits and layout: Jason Ryberg
Cover image and author photo: Allie Bird
All rights reserved. No part of this publication may be reproduced or transmitted in any form or by any means, electronic or mechanical, including photocopying, recording or by info retrieval system, without prior written permission from the author.

Día de los Muertos first appeared in *Subprimal Poetry*, Spring 2016 Issue

Thanks to the good folks at Spartan Press for supporting the St. Louis literary underground.

CONTENTS

Happy 30th / 1

Molly Crenshaw's Chicory Tea / 4

Leave Town / 7

A Rice Paper Globe Immersed In Light / 8

Kool-Aid Sandwich / 9

Flowers For the Realist / 10

Depression Diary / 12

Dia de los Muertos / 19

It Starts / 21

Revelers of the Prismatic Earth / 22

Jesse James/Robert Ford / 25

Smoking Bali Hai / 26

All the Dark Rags / 28

Note To A Former Friend / 29

First Splendor / 30

The Most Sincere Form of Criticism Is Suicide / 31

9/12/01 / 32

Blood of the Zenta / 33

Fisheye Lens / 34

Ingredients For Summoning the Rockicrucian / 35

Sock & Buskin / 36

The Avantgarden / 37

My Religion Is Chocolate / 38

Prayer Mountain / 41

Avoid Civilization / 42

Katie, Etc / 44

Thorazine Ice Cream Parlor / 45

Riddles Penultimate / 46

One More String of Pearls / 47

We Are Things in a Poet's House / 49

Ode to Mr. Enoch, Who Got Kicked in the Head / 50

Nostalgia. Pillars of Salt. / 51

People without hope don't write books.

- Flannery O'Connor

Happy 30th

And I will never grow so old again...
— Van Morrison

Life is a song your body is learning to forget.
You are misheard lyrics in this voluptuous amnesia.
A sediment of flesh, burbling,
tone-deaf, its vulgar octaves engorged
as an omer of manna writhing with
mealworms in the midlife sun.

Another bitter year ingested.

The taste of death in your mouth
wakes you nauseous and afraid.
You stretch, yawn and squabbling
madmen escape the crooked
mold of your twisted innards.
Pale horses misty on your breath.

What once beautiful
pharaoh was laid to
to rest in this
sarcophagus of bile?

A dog-headed man balances your liver
on the scales; the red cursive of your intestines strung
between his hands.

Where's the soul? he demands.
*Burgers, pills, paint chips, shit,
but no soul! Give him another year.*

The cancerous blotches
on the mattress are ruins
of Sodom etched in sweat
like cuneiform. Babel's
Tower erect in the sheets
where communication is
the jabberwock of
mating call;
idiot keening to a
blind invertebrate
boiling in its enzymes.
Is that it? she asks.
You heave a mouthful
of buttery silt.

Eyes darken,
gums recede,
strength wanes.
But wait, you see it now,
in the groggy luminance
on the chilling afterglow.
Ah, foul, ugly one. You!
The unwashed barbarian.
Make me alchemist of
your contorted affections.

Mortality measured
in friction against
the dragon of your
shoulder blades.
Hope doused
beneath the weight
of this overripe
asylum of meat.

Are you to be found within these?
For to say, *I am seeking my self*
is a misnomer. A contradiction in terms.
For to seek is the act of not having.

You are the song your body is learning to forget.

Molly Crenshaw's Chicory Tea

After reading Hohman's Pow-Wows, or Long Lost Friend

At night the black hut whispers to itself.
A dialect of haints in cicada symphonies
and innuendo of medicine dreams.

The huntress, whose face is the moon,
turns, cradling a wolfboy, and hears
the silversmiths chanting,
Great is Diana of the Ephesians!

A trailer park Aradia,
gambling with Herod
in her squaw dresses and
Cleopatra blue eyeliner,
hitchhiking the Mother Road
on the back of a butane truck.
Track-marks quote the I Ching
down her arm and the autographs
of older men still blister on her neck.

Her husband crashed his motorcycle.
The cow's milk has turned to blood.
Her firstborn has the head of a hog.
So she's gone to the conjure woman;
the rattlesnake's doula.

She followed the bloody footprints
until she realized she was following
the tracks of her own wound.

To the black cabin in the hills
where she brews her chicory tea.
The old hag is cursing moonshine.
Come in, my child.

A barn owl on the water-stained table.
Candles melted in tarantulas of wax.
You seek my chicory tea, she says.
I know the dreamtalk, rootwork, wildcraft.
I bruised the bay leaf to breed a scorpion. I've lain with
skinwalkers, the belladonna knotted in their loins. What
have I here in my satchel of gris gris? John the Conqueror
and an alligator tear? A calico cat's bone or a wasp's
stinger? Sage and jimsonweed, knot-grass,
spiderwort, mulberry, birch bark,
stinging nettle, four thieves vinegar
and ashwagandha powder.

She sips her botanical lore; vegetable gnosis
kept by hoodoo wisefolk from Ozark to Jerusalem.
Well versed in the art of healing and hexery, she proffers
various tinctures, poultices, recipe spells from her hide-
bound *Book of Useful Knowledge*. There's lavender for
serenity; wintergreen to cure headache; frankincense for
intuition.

She says, *Even Ovid, the Roman, wrote 'Now I shall tell of things that change, new being out of old.'* Cain is the mandrake, as is Micah Rood apple. Poison ivy is Rappaccini's Daughter. Bramble thorns were the crown of Christ. Acanthus vine for memory, especially doomed lovers; cypress or yew grow between their hearts. All things become of desire; legs to the fish, clothes to the ape. But I have swallowed a skeleton key, scratched a rhyme on a Freemason Bible, turned thrice and burned it black. Now my womb is the world.

Leave Town (an STL Weather Report)

Cut and run.
That's the sign you were born under.
Everyone you know has slit their wrist with a *fleur-de-lis*.
If you stay, will you join them?

A Rice Paper Globe Immersed in Light

A cricket sings her kōan among the peach trees,
the breadth of jade heaven within a Buddha's laugh.

Laozi stands with one foot in the yellow river,
holding the Eight Immortals as trigrams in his
cinnabar box.

The waxwing alights on a bamboo pavilion
where the stone monkey rests his head under
the maple blossom empire in October's bed.

Kool-Aid Sandwich
For Ariel Pink
(to be read in any direction)

neon   beach   guitar

     arcade   mezcal   hairspray

         disembodied
taco   beatnik   TV

    boombox   drunken   static

underwater   synth   lipgloss

      disco   ill   Hollywood

Nosferatu   jacuzzi   symphony

     '80s   outer space

haunted   cassette   glitter

     falsetto   coke   angels

denim   blowjob   graffiti

    kung-fu cartoon   killer

nightlife   freak   antenna

Flowers for the Realist

A miktam

If we spoke the language of romance then our tongue would be our pen. But our tongue has crept like arsenic into every well from which we drink. It has poisoned gratitude with its condescension and starved benevolence with ridicule. We drag our sweet inversions of the truth through the marketplace, temper festering like an open sore – too fearful to buy, too envious to sell – as we speak famine and horde what little thanks we have to give, thinking ourselves robbed of what we do not possess. Each new idea strikes a whetstone against the tongue, sharpened to Damascus steel, it flits down S. Grand in broad daylight, slashing the vocal cords of any corner gadfly braying, *Have you seen the corpse of Sayat Nova lying open to the sun in the littered streets of Kabul as doves flutter from his bullet holes? Have you seen child soldiers dragging museums of rubble through a mirage of Liberty Street?* The tongue is a scimitar on the coffee table. An insult sheathed under a hilt of regret. Remember, pain is the teacher, not the lesson. An apology is a scar. So I let the pen speak for me. Because it is less restless. More certain. Secure enough to not be so easily offended. It is not so prideful in its redemption of the gift the tongue has forfeit. *Silence!* says the pen, *You who claim to be a humble quill-driver. Who thinks the hydrangea blooms in his throat. Who thinks his tongue is a bookmark in time. I've dealt with your kind before. You common haggler of blotch and smeared paper! Flogger of cheap semantics! Despiser, distorter, denier of all human relationships! You obscure knowledge and call it artistry! You wallow in doubt and publish the suicide of your own mind! You conceited wastrel! You've gone to bed with your imagination and left every woman unrequited and alone. The years haven't made you stronger, just less tender. You've befriended books and ignored your loved ones. You've chosen intellect over experience. The rhetorical over the real. You, like Tukaram, claim you're 'looking for a poem that says everything so you won't have to write anymore.' Bullshit! You've walked a thousand leagues in falsehood in hopes that one step might be true. You're a junkie, plain and simple, chasing the dregs of your thwarted ambition. Hiding insecurity behind insincerity, you mock what you can't attain to gratify your envy, unable to admit that You are the thing you fear. You're not as clever as you think. Not as in control as you'd like. Not as close to the end as you need to be. You only open your mouth to close mine.*

Depression Diary

SUN

*I threw away my first Beatles LP
when I learned all you need isn't love.
It's trust.*

MON

*I bought my first Rolling Stones record
when I learned love is not innocent.
And neither am I.*

TUE

The temptation to exist stirs up paradox.

WED

Nature can be Art, but Art cannot be Nature.

THURS

I've been blinded by all I can see.

FRI

It's nice to do things because I want to do them.
Not because I want to want to do them.

SAT

I want me today
when I'm not around
no one can make them alright
no one can say I'm better not around
but all these feelings again is a lie

Día de los Muertos

From *Subprimal Poetry*, Spring 2016 Issue

24th & Mission – where virgins appear with bloodied lips, lifting their puebla blouses, the Spanish quarters of Telegraph and Castro, as colorful deaths. The Festival of Altars comes gleaming like maharajahs along empty bottle offerings. Mexican lanterns. Holy Spirit. Floating goldmines. Bodies like gnarled caskets raise the 13 Standards while fruit hat chiquitas in suede dresses carry dried flowers to the hooded groom, swinging fuming censers that hint at Orient gardens. In the streets there are salamanders, shedding the dark as they go wanting after the sacred flame. From the Nubian depths – its charnel portals – they step through as mediums down the tunnel of days, fed by prehistoric winds that howl with saurian nightmares. The drumbeat. Chupacabras. Below there are gantesses who offer draughts of the blue agave that go down like devil's breath, reeling with dust, with camphor and iodine...yerba santa baptisms. Call out the flaxen wives of the boneyard, black roses in their teeth. Escort them aboard subterranean ferries past bishops and sorcerers and pale little girls with their hair in marigolds, to Aztecs in coyote skin who jostle together to become smoke and joss paper. A link of dancers leads them on to a red mesa, the haunt of the ghast and cold-kissed Persephones, where the hanged kings, the twice-born fathers, leave their adobe houses to join in the gay confusion hid in Venetian masks and maidens' kisses. They bow to the pieces of Osiris found by children, torn apart like piñatas, spices, toys and lapis lazuli, sprinkled like kosher salt over the doorstep. The long road ponders a scythe. Sandmen line the catacombs. To the Mission Dolores Basilica made of ivory speaking in sutras. Carvings, morphs, making love to one another. Your god-bitten towers pointing. San Francisco: a wreckage of gargoyles crashing into the sky. Here there are feasts in the cemetery. The weeping willow women in their red girdles kneel in adoration at the altar cloth, laid with cakes of light and plates of quince and grails of strange wine touched with ash. The olden ones dine on the gilded tomb. And after their suppers the matadors in their capes lay gifts of Arabian hash and de la rosa candies at the gates of the soil, a Star of David carved on the headstone with a serpent's tooth. And the Witch of Words, one of filigree and manners, spins tales of glamor around her seven pillars, while her handmaids pave the way holding portraits of the blessed: Dred Scott, Cuauhtémoc, Frida Kahlo, Geronimo, Benito Juárez, Gloria Anzaldúa, Katherine Dunham, Josephine Baker and more.

IT STARTS WHEN YOU CARE TO ACT
WHEN YOU DO IT AGAIN
AFTER THEY SAY NO
WHEN YOU SAY WE
AND KNOW WHO YOU MEAN
AND EACH DAY
YOU MEAN ONE MORE

Revelers of the Prismatic Earth

Your branches inscribe the dawn
into fierce mosaics of light!
Sketches of infinite veinwork,
the body of a Sandoz Odin
hanging from the genetic
Tree of Life.

The I stands ajar.
The way is open.
Come and become.

Torment us, blessed arteries!
Murmur your seductions, you
vessels of unseen anatomy
who are aloof to my caresses.
You, Green Maternity!

Speak to me! Show some
sign of your affection to
this star-swathed traveler
bedecked in the flowering
boughs of my imaginings.

They are the limbs and fruit
of generations. Multitudes
stretching back from my
parents to Antediluvia.

My ancestry traced through
dew-sweet canals beyond forever,
on and on, a web of fractal patterns.
Neuro-genesis. Psycho-archeology.
Falling deeper, deeper back, toward
the dawn of consciousness, past souls uncountable,
undulating like rainbow
shoals of starfish.

We are One
for a moment
and I knew their names!

Mary, who fled Smyrna's Great Fire
to be born John in Yonkers and drive
a Sherman tank through the Battle
of Herrlisheim, to K'uru who hunted
mastodon in Gondwana and worshiped
the cave bear, to the New Awakenings,
astral pink in their chakras adorned
with ivy and linen, dancing in a
crystal city of nine gates.

These visions housed in runes of skin
appear within their fathomless depths,
their flanks panting in summers veiled,
turn my fragile yearning against the
musky incense from nature's fertility,
a chorus of perfume.

Honor your chemistry. It is the movement of centuries. Revelers of this prismatic earth that flow within you; passing gondolas in a stream of white fire.

JESSE JAMES:
If I'm not sick, then how can I get better?

ROBERT FORD:
There is no cure for the truth.

Smoking Bali Hai

I beat my chest like a kettle drum
until it gave the darkness a pulse.
Ran with teenage Mercuries in Retrograde,
electricity in their pores, the loft-dwellers at
Arsenal and Locust, thespians scared famous,
musicians under house arrest, PMers, strays,
a tribe of hedonists, rabid for use, pushing life
through the stem of their bodies like a lit fuse.
They always come in threes,
smoking Bali Hai.
Sucking off their corkscrew brains,
frustrated in a pink hotel, breaking
the Seventh Seal in protein that
mocks me in my efforts as still
they do rise and slough off their
madhouse vanities in tangled sheets,
where hot springs well up in who
they were the night before.
They are obsessed with last things
and smoking Bali Hai.
Half-naked bingers nailed to a microphone
calvary, weeping alcohol. Detoxed, under the rug,
chasing their tail around the hole again,
the absence of a noun. Like them, do I burn with
lukewarm vengeance because the contemporary

is temporary, but the present has no limit? Do I gorge
myself on pleasure until I'm sick with jagged decadence?
Or am I smuggling misery into every party with a
prosthetic hunger for a careless kiss or vital
piercing to rampant dimensions of
thoughtless salvation? I shall refer to myself as *"it."*
For it has been eaten alive by meaninglessness. Arrayed
in Urban Outfits, they wear Converse sneakers; jean
jackets; lace leggings; leaving long-distance phone calls,
dinner reservations, half-burned notes, spare hotel keys.
They pay a lot of money to look like they're poor,
smoking Bali Hai.
Still, I am waiting to see them:
wrapped in the folds of the Chrysler dawn
by twenty-seven Virgos in the chilled drops
of Ophelia's anesthesia, rolled like Turkish carpet
in the never-ending west.

All the Dark Rags

Well, you must be Joan of Arc, otherwise your cradle
wouldn't still be in flames and the voice of God wouldn't
keep telling you, *You're on your own* in French. I
heard you moved back to Arimathea, Missouri where
the Archangel Gabriel laid down on the railroad tracks.
Where the next whiskey shot leads along a rosary's beads
to that clapboard convent between your breasts; the
middle of nowhere.

You retreat to the county line, Gog & Magog, where you've
rallied an army of admirers to protect you from that boy
who swore he'd be your dauphin. You drowned all his
records, along with your hope, in a burlap bag. Tired of
his cryptic tales and doomsday ballads, you threw his
reed pipe in the creek. Now you only sleep with a knife
and dream of battles lost. When you broke like pottery,
you said you joined the cracks with gold.

A messenger who is the message, jackrabbiting the lonely
dogwoods with only your faith strapped to your back
and a bandana full of centurion's nails and a ripped photo
tucked between the pages of Fox's Book of Martyrs. You
said you can't hear cathedral bells over the obscenity of
traffic. Neither can anyone hear the farmer's cry when
the hound is at his rooster's neck or when his daughter
falls into the quarry or when smoke blots out the horizon.
You think you've found a companion in isolation. Really
you've dug your bed in a field nearer to heaven, but further
from everything else. A parable on the edge of time. You say
love was defeated. It simply did not fight.

Note to a Former Friend

You could help me out, you could slow me down,
you could show me things that otherwise I would just pass by.

While listening to *House of Gold* I had a vision of you
in the Bay Area sitting under an archway of gardenias.
Espresso beans on a plate beside you, as well as a lemon
sliced in fourths. Your peppermint dress, offset by
seashells, turning into the weary coastal percentage like
a Rasta mermaid. Holi dust smeared on your forehead
and I could see through a circus of clouds, down the
ways of iridescent pollen, you were making a funny face,
tempting the sun to earth to demand its fare share down
the long tie-dye passage of your voracious smile, for no
one can wear Haight-Ashbury like a Chinatown dragon.
Even the ornery Pacific isn't fooled into condensing on
your lashes.

First Splendor
(Intensive Care)

A plastic flower grows
inside your chest

Clear tubes purify
heavy fluids to infinite vapor

Light cleanses every wrinkle
memories on a wheel

Dried rose, ripened fig,
a fringe of delicate scars

The arithmetic of grief
against our inventory of love

The cloying odor of despair,
decaying summer lilac

The rest is inescapable

The Most Sincere Form of Criticism Is Suicide

Then I saw myself.
I was dead.
Naked.
In a bathtub
on sphinx paws.
I crouched by the
rim of the tub
and fondled my
wet hair.
My neck hung limp
and heavy as a baby's.
A note on the
floor reads only:
Messy, isn't it?
And I said to my other self,
Yes, he writes. *But only
when the spirit moves him.
And he does not divine it
from the whispered lips of
his muse. It comes upon him in fits.*

9/12/01

Washington hired five men
to chop down the cherry tree.
First they blamed it on Muhammed,
now they blame it on you and me.

Blood of the Zenta

But his blood was not spilled in vain; the animals came and lapped it up. And with just one taste, the beasts of the field stood upright and began to speak blasphemies. With the intelligence of men, the rats and stray dogs began to preach the message of the Zenta. Even the birds of the air fill the skies with Braille. The carrion crows soared overhead and screamed *Traitors!*
Because the Word in him could not be silenced. They wrapped their babe in silks handled by lions and weaned him on honeycomb from the mouth of the asp. For the child hath lain in the nest of the komodo. He will break the rod of the oppressor and teach the mule to speak. The cockerel shall sigh in an excess of desire when it remembers him, saying, *See the place where he fell. They who write their confessions upon it shall be the walkers between worlds. Not without a wound in the spirit shall I leave this flesh. And I shall be welcomed into the open arms of the Zenta.*

Fisheye Lens

How perverse it is
that we feel the need
to take pictures constantly
to prove to our friends
we're alive.

In a life made of photographs,
once you embalm time
you make the whole world
your tomb.

And to hold to every piece
is to let go of movement.

Ingredients for Summoning the Rockicrucian: Magic Rites of the American Teenager

I. A vinyl album; preferably the Brian Jonestown Massacre, preferably scratched.

II. A bottle of Johnnie Walker; preferably Black Label.

III. A book of poetry; preferably Rimbaud, Genet or Lorca.

IV. A damp parka; preferably slept in, outside, on the grass.

V. Cold pizza.

VI. A hippie lighter; preferably one with a skull, peace sign or Hebrew letter on it.

VII. A stick of incense; preferably Nag Champa or bubblegum.

VIII. A work of art; preferably a band poster, tie-dye tapestry or bikini centerfold.

IX. A personal item of great sentimental value; preferably one given by an ex.

Note: all ritualists involved in this summoning must sit in a circle and attune themselves by repeating the following, *The first rule of becoming an artist is 'forget your name.' And the second is like it, 'call yourself by everyone else's.*

Sock & Buskin

What is the piece trying to tell us? our high school theater teacher asked. The assignment was a two-to-three minute skit, non-verbal, in which you express who you really are. Before I began, I handed out a red solo cup to each of my classmates. At the end of my act, accompanied by the song *Anemone*, I stood on a table and held an empty wine bottle over my head. I tilted it forward, symbolically pouring it out above them. Some kids raised their cups to be filled. Others didn't. One persnickety member of the drama club, a teacher's pet, raised his hand during the Q&A. *Um, I didn't really feel it, you know? He didn't make me want to lift my cup. So I didn't,* he complained. *Good,* I replied. *A performance is what happens to you. You can either accept it, or reject it. Your cup is your cup. What you chose to do with it has nothing to do with me. I can only pour mine out.*

The Avantgarden
For Ern Malley

The blue-skinned child buries his clock among the
watermelon. His mother has two sons, but only one
breast. She looks at him, her eyes glowworms, and says,
*You must choose. Which one shall be fed? One is pure
genius, the other, a hoax. The one who survives is the one
you believe in.* He says, *You killed my brother.* She says,
You're an only child. She has six arms. In one she carries
a black swan...in one, a white nectarine...in another, a
coiled serpent...in another, a sacred lotus...an Egyptian
ankh rests above her navel. The rest he cannot interpret.
Fates scribbled by a left-handed god.
She cut her hair and he went insane.
Left with a midnight forest in his hands.
By the goldfish pond the blue-skinned child
carries his face inside a book, pages folding
in accordion staircases.

My Religion is Chocolate

I believed in that first cup of water right after
an ice cream cone.

I believed nicknames were more important than
real names.

I believed in choking down sushi to impress your friends.

I believed in Wes Anderson and Michel Gondry
movie marathons.

I believed in sharing a pint of Bailey's Irish Cream
on the courthouse steps.

I believed in *The Tao of Pooh* overdue at the library.

I believed in eating a mason jar full of raisins under
a Christmas tree.

I believed in flirting with a girl by writing on
airplane napkins.

I believed in getting attacked by geese for breadcrumbs.

I believed in my mother's voice reading me bible verses
at bedtime.

I believed in a crazy old fisherman with a harpoon who dangled a dead squid in my face and squirted me with ink.

I believed in dinner reservations under the name *Houdini*.

I believed in big-ass headphones.

I believed in that part of sex, the best part, you know, when your neck snaps back at the end and you think, *Ope! That's it! I really did it this time! Now I'm paralyzed!* But then you're relieved when you find you can move again.

I believed in mix CDs, even the ones I can't bear to listen to anymore:
The Greatest - Cat Power
Passing Afternoon - Iron & Wine
Casimir Pulaski Day - Sufjan Stevens
Our House - Crosby, Stills, Nash & Young
Diamond Day - Vashti Bunyan
Love My Way - The Psychedelic Furs
You Could Make A Killing - Aimee Mann
Ceremony - New Order
Sunflower - Low
Comptine d'un autre été: l'après-midi - Yann Tiersen
Care of Cell 4 - The Zombies
Natural's Not In It - Gang of Four

Whole Wide World - Wreckless Eric
Phone Call - Jon Brion
I'm Not Saying - Nico
Hello, Rain - The Softies
Rebel, Rebel - David Bowie
Song For A Blue Guitar - Red House Painters
The Only Living Boy In New York - Paul Simon

I believed in bittersweet cocoa on your lips under an Afghan quilt on a rainy afternoon.

Prayer Mountain

You can practice the presence of God
when you find an arrowhead in the gravel.
Your purpose is not in what you do.
It's what you do with what you do.
We raise our hands in worship
to remind us they are empty.

Avoid Civilization

That is the cry you hear the loudest, over the deafening
void in its metal sleep, over the clamorous solitude among
its crowded urbanites, you hear the call, *come away, come
away!,* over vertical colonies of electricity, over smog
reclined on limescale erosion as a blonde nude in repose,
you can avoid civilization in the midst of a city, for New
York is Old York – Ill, Decrepit, Ancient York – and Thrice-
Great Chicago, the Patriarch, brutalized all his sons, while
Los Angeles is in withdrawal some feral thing in your heart
kicks against the ziggurat of your ribcage with the hind legs
of a newborn gazelle, Eden pierced on its antlers, bounding
across rough and swaying grasslands that roll toward the
shores of ecstasy behind your wallpaper at night, serenaded
by fang and talon clawing their bloody rhythm through
the verge of your humanity for intercession with a primal
wilderness deep within, tabla and djembe, a heretic's psalm
inhaled through untamed lungs, enjambed in the percussion
of tumbling limbs, a stampede of wildebeest, a singing stone
calling out over totems and beasts, over formless waters,
the Logos calls you home, come away from the vignettes
of men, come away from their Ithaca stacked pretend in
concrete ecclesiastic, rumbling ever onward on the backs
of the innocent, swoon with heady gluttonies, missing their
cue at the whim of an unseen narrator – cruel, indifferent
with leviathan purpose – return to the lost country you are,
borderless, intangible landscape tepid on the precipice of
waking nothing, return to your far-wandering thoughts that
take flight as neither crow nor man and bring you to caverns

of beautiful madness smeared like neolithic paintings inside your head that you may feast upon its mysteries that even as you grow older you become wary what if everyone you've ever met was just the thousand faces of the clockwork that runs this ancient machine

Katie, Etc.

Fall softly,
and look into red canyons
colored by red crayons.
I could just see the side of her face
edged against a mildewed screen
bleached with grief.
After counting the countless
gray hairs of the universe,
I can assure you
she was more
than that.

Thorazine Ice Cream Parlor
To Remedios Varo

After the revolution, maraschino syrup flows
down the marble steps of the capitol.
El Presidente hangs from the flagpole, tarred and
feathered in hot butterscotch and marshmallow, as we
sang *Long live the Nouveau Republic!* His seventh wife,
Violante, in her drawing room, posing nude for Goya.
Cassiel, the swordsman, his white shirt billowing, rides
his licorice-black stallion through the great hall and
tramples her. Her lover, Santiago, chases Estella, the
chambermaid, over glass shards from a broken chandelier
on the floor. He slips; cracks his neck like hazelnut
biscotti. Behind amaretto curtains, warm in peach and
gold pecan, Raul, the beggar boy, covers an ornate
painting in excrement. Baba, the dog, finds a birdcage
full of wishbones near a headless alabaster bust.
The generals in the kitchen are filling their pockets with
silverware. Estella tricks them into the oven and bakes
them into a souffle; breasts of meringue. Dr. Dulce runs
into the jungle wearing a lady's dress. The People's Army
overthrow the mansions of the rich; their palaces looted;
their chocolate doubloons thrown off the balcony in
the pastel shambles of Old Town. Widows and orphans
play in their bedchambers of saffron paint on buttermilk
neutrals. Pleasure temples of gelato overgrown with
the spiny octopi of aloe vera, banyan tree curlicues. the
ceiling livid with squawking, surrealist Macaws. The
coffin-maker enjoys a sorbet of mango, coconut and lime.

Riddles Penultimate

A green tigress prowls, smokey-eyed, through the brass. The Hammond organ hollers darkly from a nickel juke as polyester divas clap over old beer and leather to hear the muted trumpet. The chromium flume blows black and blue, feelings scraped along gravel, aluminum cans, cigar butts. The gold-tooth gambler said the word *jazz* comes from *jasmine,* after the perfume worn by prostitutes where Jelly Roll played piano. It moves him to sport sharp threads, the pompadour, buoyant heeled, rugs cut with fancy footwork, his luck greased down and shining through two-tone spats, his bossanova alligators.

One More String of Pearls

One more drink in lethe steeped.
Saturday is a taste of eternity.
The last drop spills. *If you
believe in me, I will believe in you.*

One more glance thrown like a
roman candle at her blue china smile.
Another pale idol, a woman's name
that's called my name, giving herself
to unremarkable men whose hearts
are revolving doors.

One more time, cry *immanentize
the eschaton!* Awakened again
by your circadian clock, we lost
a lifetime in a moment; a fifth
season, the distance of my penis,
spread in crushed velvet.

One more green-line girl who can't
stutter when she sings in the closet.
The joys of uncertainty. Out for a
meal at another's expense. You say
*the world doesn't fit me when
I chose to wear it. So I go naked
through the years asking, quem
quaeritis?*

One more handkerchief filled
with your swears. What I've said
deadens my legs. Silence warms
the snowbank. This whole city
enters you. Once more, my sweet
Saint Louis, I love you. But don't
have the heart to die in you.

We Are Things in a Poet's House

The harmony of your pursed lips forms a tourniquet
between the weeks we are together
and the years we'll spend apart.

Friendship is a shard of glass that reflects everyone;
behaviors that rhyme with feeling.

They give me lemon egg drop soup and Debussy sheet music,
even though they know I can't play.
Objectification of sincerity.
They delight in creating me.

Running my thoughts through your hair like a comb,
teasing out braided moments, the spaces most dear to me
a little north of comprehension. Their mouths are full of light.

Depression is a blank. An addendum of bruises
underlined in the middle of the space you leave behind.
In the space that was once an object. This poem ends on
someone's anniversary, burrowed in your oriental rug,
the colors fall asleep.

Ode to Mr. Enoch, Who Got Kicked in the Head

Dead barbies in the manila envelope. That, and a rusted bowie knife in the top drawer. Sister Sue is afraid to clean his hospice cell. For how do you explain all these moths clustered around the argyle? The Greek letters spelled out in baked beans? Or drawings of Hermes shaking hands with Thoth in Alexandria? Like Balaam's donkey that kept him from the destroyer on the road, good old Mr. Enoch's horse plowed a field in his right temple, where a crop of fiery-wheeled, many-eyed elohim float among the rye. He remembers the future in a malted milk; the last indigo child stands alone outside its triple-body. They do not marry for they can no longer die. He hears the voice of the tyrannosaurus in the petroleum; a high priestess harbored deep in his ear-bone, who told him we don't live on the outer crust of the earth but underneath it, on the inside of our globe. The sun is its molten core. So when we look 'out' at the night sky we're looking in at constellations of our own energy. The universe is finite. And five sided. He sees Dogon shamans resurrected by UFOs that swim through aqua-lucent depths of space like a race of gill-men from the Dog Star, Sirius B. His callused hands clad in a tinge of grime and toil, yet nothing is beyond his grasp. The harmonics of sacred geometry appear to him in pea pods growing on the porch trellis; the music of mathematics; the phi ratio; platonic solids in his copper kettle. Since atheists replaced God with a clock, evolution is the watched pot that never boils. But nobody listens. They know Mr. Enoch ain't right. *That's alright,* he'd say, *you ain't you.* Some of the world's greatest poets work in gas stations. Only you'd never know, because they don't write anything down.

Nostalgia. Pillars of Salt.

I wanted to live forever.
At least twenty-seven years.
Any more than that is failure.

The songs on the radio ask me
what is happiness?
I don't know.
But it only lasts
two minutes and
thirty seconds.

Denmark Laine is a St. Louis poet and novelist whose work has been featured on Fox 2 KTVI, *Subprimal Poetry*, STL TV Live, the St. Louis Poetry Slam, *Eleven Magazine* and *Bad Jacket*. He is a graduate of Southern Illinois University Edwardsville with a Bachelor of Fine Arts in Theatre. He is the author of *The Gods of Autumn, Exile On Cherokee Street* and *Smalltown Kings*.

This project was made possible, in part, by generous support from the Osage Arts Community.

Osage Arts Community provides temporary time, space and support for the creation of new artistic works in a retreat format, serving creative people of all kinds — visual artists, composers, poets, fiction and nonfiction writers. Located on a 152-acre farm in an isolated rural mountainside setting in Central Missouri and bordered by ¾ of a mile of the Gasconade River, OAC provides residencies to those working alone, as well as welcoming collaborative teams, offering living space and workspace in a country environment to emerging and mid-career artists. For more information, visit us at www.osageac.org

Osage Arts Community

www.ingramcontent.com/pod-product-compliance
Lightning Source LLC
Chambersburg PA
CBHW020634130526
44591CB00043BA/642